WAITING

on

GOD

Please Note:

This paperback was created due to overwhelming demand
by those who had bought the Kindle Version.
The *WAITING on GOD* portion is relatively short.
The sample 1st chapter of *BE STILL* is a true bonus.
This was not, however intended to be a paperback.
I have priced the paperback as LOW as I possibly can in order
to make it available for those who insisted on a printed version.

Cherie Hill

WAITING on GOD

At any given point in time, you'll find yourself waiting on "something." You might be waiting on something very small, or you could be waiting on something that will change the course of your life. Either way, the "waiting place" is the hardest place. Dr. Seuss described our *feelings* about the "waiting place" best:

You can get so confused
that you'll start in to race
down long wiggled roads at a break-necking pace
and grind on for miles across weirdish wild space,
headed, I fear, toward a most useless place.
The Waiting Place . . .
(Dr. Seuss, *Oh, the Places You'll Go!*)

We find ourselves easily consumed with despair and hopelessness in our waiting places. Uncertainty and lack of control can get the best of us. We tend to view the "waiting place" as Dr. Seuss did . . . as a "confusing, fearful, and useless place." But it is not . . . unless we're not walking with God. If we're trusting in God, we can be certain that there is no such thing as Him being "almost" sovereign. If we say we have "faith," then we must live like we do. And the "waiting place" is precisely the "place" God uses to examine our faith and see if it is genuine. The "waiting place" is where He purifies us, allowing the impurities of our spirit to come to the surface. The "waiting place" is part of the process. And we can trust that God will not allow us to remain in the "waiting place" one moment longer than it takes to accomplish His purposes for them. He wouldn't have you waiting if there weren't something to wait for. He wouldn't refine you if He didn't know He was purifying gold. But it's when He's holding us to the fire, when the pain and suffering is more than we can bear, our heart cries out with questions that beg answers.

It's in our most desperate, darkest hour that we cry out countless questions to God:

"Why are you allowing this?"
"What is the purpose in this?"
"Are you there?" . . . *"Do you care?"*

But you see, for all the questions we have for God, He has questions for us too . . . and as our heart pours out tears to heaven, the answer from God sometimes comes in the form of a question . . .

Where is your faith?

Luke 8:28 (NLT)

———oo&o&oo———

What we find, as we ponder upon that question, is that our "faith" has grown "weary" in the waiting. You pray, but God doesn't seem to be listening. You trust Him, but He appears to be letting you down. You believe His Word, but His promises are coming up seemingly empty in your life. You seek, but do not find . . . you knock, but no one is answering. If God is doing anything at all in your life . . . *you can't see it.* The fight of faith intensifies, as it appears that not only is God running late . . . *He may not even show up at all.* By the looks of things, God's too busy with the rest of the world and He's not paying attention to your life at all. With each passing hour, your Spirit grows weary . . . in the "waiting."

My eyes are straining
to see your Promises come true.
When *will you comfort me?*
Psalm 119:82 (NLT)

I am exhausted from crying for help;
my throat is parched.
My eyes are swollen with weeping,
waiting *for my God to help me.*
Psalm 69:3 (NLT)

It's been said that the hardest part of faith is the last half hour. Waiting on God tests us like nothing else does. When we're experiencing overwhelming confusion, we can be certain that deliverance is just around the corner. The problem is that *we give up* just before *God shows up*.

In the *Screwtape Letters*, by C.S. Lewis, the senior demon gives his "junior" tempter a lesson . . . and we get a glimpse of how the enemy works in our "waiting place":

"Whatever he says, let his inner resolution be not
to bear whatever comes him, but to bear it
'for a reasonable period'—and let the reasonable
period be shorter than the trial is likely to last.
It need not be much shorter; in attacks on patience,
chastity, and fortitude, ***the fun is to make the man***
yield just when (had he but known it)
relief was almost in sight."

We tend to "yield" when relief was almost in sight. In the darkness, we tend to give up just before the Light breaks through. Charles Spurgeon once said, *"The wilderness is the way to Canaan. Defeat prepares us for victory. The darkest hour of the night precedes the dawn."* Remember that in your darkest hour . . . one way or another dawn *is* coming and there will be Light.

We love God's grace, but we don't like His watch. His calendar appears to be astonishingly different than the ones we hang on our walls. We're not sure He's managing time, or our lives, very well at all. If we're not seeing our situation through God's eyes in the mundane, seemingly empty times of our lives, we will grow weary in the waiting and our faith may fail.

What we don't realize in our times of desperation is that if God is guiding our steps, if He's directing our lives, then He has allowed us to be brought into the very valley in which we cry out for mercy. The fact is, God has permitted the circumstances that have brought us to our knees, and He has done so with a plan *and* a purpose.

You see, there's a BIG difference between "being still" and "doing nothing." When God appears to have escorted you into His "waiting room," you can be certain that He doesn't want you "doing nothing" . . . He wants you "being still." He has a plan, and in order for Him to work, He needs you trusting Him . . .

completely.

But the enemy fills us with the lies that we must take action . . . take matters into our own hands. The enemy whispers, "God's Word can't be relied upon, He can't be trusted . . . *you* have to do something! You've waited long enough! God isn't going to show up!" But God's strong, still small voice replies, "*Wait on Me . . . I will save you . . . I will deliver you . . . I hold your life (every detail) in the palms of My hands.*" The enemy wants you to believe that the "waiting place" is a "wasted place," but faith says something different . . . it says, *"Trust God and rest in Him . . . wait in faith."*

While you're waiting, God wants you praying, drawing nearer to Him, and resting in the peace that He provides in the midst of a raging storm. As you wait, God strengthens you because you begin to realize that God IS at work . . . *He's growing your faith and He's purifying your heart.* And faith is rarely grown with anything other than overwhelming circumstances, and typically not found in any place other than the "waiting place." There's no other way to purify gold than by the fire; it's part of the process . . . and it's *necessary*.

God knows what He's doing.

God has brought you to a place of helplessness and hopelessness, so that you know when you're in need . . . **He is ALL you need.** In whatever you're waiting for right now, it may appear that God is absent. But you must lay hold of God's Promises that assure you:

> *No ear heard, no eye seen,*
> *a God like you who works*
> ***for those who wait for him.***
> Isaiah 64:4 (MSG)

God has not forgotten you . . . he has not abandoned you in your time of desperation. He often works best in your brokenness . . . a humble heart is more moldable in His hands. Stop worrying about the details . . . quit trying to figure it all out—God knows what He's doing. ***He's in control . . . even when life isn't.*** Trust that when your world seems to be falling apart . . . *it's really* *just falling into place in the hands of your Almighty loving God.* Trust. Wait. Rest. God's help is on the way. Wait in faith . . . and don't let "doubt" get the best of you.

———oo◦●◦oo———

Like an uninvited guest, "Doubt" shows up at the most inopportune times—just when we grab hold of our faith and grasp on to whatever is left of Hope . . . Doubt comes knocking at the door. But, when we find Doubt knocking . . . we should be sure and let Faith answer.

The truth is that as we wait, we can't help but wonder why God isn't showing up when we think He should. And Doubt can get the best of us. We assume that if we're walking with God, we should see Seas parted, giants taken down, and countless miracles that cause us to walk on water. But, God promised us something much different. He said that in this world we would have trouble—we should count on it (see John 16:33). It's when trouble comes that we must place our trust in God's sovereignty, supernatural power, love, mercy, and grace . . .

but that's not what happens.

In our times of desperation, when we've been waiting longer than we think we should have to, Doubt takes over and begins to wreak havoc in our souls. We find ourselves between the walls of the Red Sea . . . assured that God has rescued us in the past, but filled with doubt, as we see the treacherous waters ready to come crashing in on us and an encroaching army ready to attack. Time is running out. The situation seems "doubtful." It appears "unlikely" that God will show up "this time."

We must remember in our most desperate moments in life that it is God who has often led us to the very place we cry out from . . . the "waiting place" . . . the place where we face impossibilities. And God has led us to this place to teach us a much needed lesson in our walk of faith—*we cannot deliver ourselves from a crisis that God himself has orchestrated.* Too often, it is by His design that we are in the "waiting place" . . . in the midst of an overwhelming situation. We so quickly become focused upon the seemingly insurmountable circumstances, instead of our supernatural God.

The outcome of our trial depends upon one thing: *Our faith in God.* And it's the "waiting place" that tests our faith and ultimately strengthens us so that we have a testimony that says, *"My God is faithful."* When we're put to the *ultimate test of faith*, when we've been "waiting" and nothing is happening . . . we find giant issues facing us, high seas of affliction, and the evil of principalities and powers seeking to destroy us. It is then that we must totally cast ourselves on God's Promises and slam the door on Doubt. We must decide to confidently walk forward, as the walls of the Sea seem eager to take us down and it appears God has hung us out to dry. We must stand upon the faith we profess and declare that God is bigger.

> *"The goal of living a life of faith is never*
> *to go against God, but to go with Him.*
> *It isn't just about getting what you want,*
> *it's about seeking God's best,*
> *then trusting Him with His answer."*
> –Linda Evans Shepherd

Whatever you're going through, God is in it. He has allowed the circumstances that have brought you to this "waiting place," and He's increasing your faith by threatening to destroy it. If you are walking in faith, God has ordered your steps—He has put you where you are. He has good reason for it . . . *you are being tested.* And your faith must be tested because, in the words of P.B.S. Pinchback,

"Faith isn't Faith,
until it's all you're holding on to!"

It's *beyond* the doubt, as you stand still, holding your peace, and staying focused upon your sovereign God, you will find that God's deliverance doesn't come through something you do, say, or pray . . . *but through your faith.* And your faith comes by way of God's grace . . . which is often *disguised.*

———oo⁀●‿oo———

While we're "waiting," we can't help but question if God is who He really says He is. There are moments, sometimes years, when our faith falls short and we're consumed with the possibility that God either doesn't care or He really isn't there. But, we don't discover the power of God's immeasurable love and power by standing in mountaintop moments. We find God's undeniable presence in our darkest day, our hardest nights, and in the deepest valleys; it's when we realize that *nothing short of a miracle from God can save us.* It's when God must show up or it's all over—that's when we find God. His Light shines brightest in the darkness and His love is more powerful in our emptiness. His mighty hand is most evident when we're in a lion's den, facing giants, or our lives are threatened by a raging storm. When all hope seems gone, we find God . . . in our "waiting place" . . . ever–present, embracing us with His unfailing love, and pouring down His endless grace . . . which is *always* sufficient.

You see, you can't say that you truly "trust God," unless you've had your faith put to the test . . . unless you've had the opportunity to "distrust" Him. You can't say that you're praying for God's will and trusting in His timing if you're not willing to "wait." It's when we're in the "waiting place" that a Divine opportunity knocks. Our disappointments are God's appointments. He's arranged this meeting place to have some "one on one" time with you, in order to show you things about yourself and your faith that are critical for the rest of your journey. God knows what you want, but loves you far too much . . . *so He gives you what you need.* And He knows you need to remain in the "waiting place," until His work is done. Be assured, every difficulty you face, in every waiting place, you're being given the chance to trust in the things unseen and to be abundantly blessed:

> *Blessed are those who believe*
> *without seeing me.*
> John 20:29 (NLT)

> *God blesses those who patiently*
> *endure testing and temptation.*
> James 1:12 (NLT)

When you're "waiting" and God seems nowhere to be found, it's His grace that upholds you when you're too weak to carry on. And it's His Word that your faith will need to depend upon. In our most overwhelming moments of life, we will need something to hold on to; and if it's not the Promises of God, we'll find ourselves grabbing hold of anything and everything in this world to save us. Yet, one way or another, we'll find that *only Jesus saves.* The raging storm in your life is God's grace disguised . . .

He's giving you the opportunity to see Him calm it.

Every "waiting place" is God's way of *preparing you to see Himself face to face* . . . to witness miracles beyond all you can hope for or imagine (see Ephesians 3:20).

In your "waiting place," while you're declaring your trust in God, it may be difficult to accept that God has allowed you to face such dire circumstances. Your faith may get shaken to its core when you realize that if God is who He says He is, then He has permitted the pain and suffering you are going through each day. But, it's when you're down to nothing . . . *God is up to something.* His grace disguised as pain, tears, emptiness of soul, and endless waiting is bringing you to a place of witnessing Him in ways you never imagined. His grace disguised in your life will reveal His constant *presence*, His mighty *power*, His perfect *provision*, and His abundant *peace,* as He strengthens your faith **in** the "waiting place."

When you're facing great uncertainty, stuck somewhere in the land "in-between," waiting on God to show up, grab hold of the opportunity to trust Him . . . *even when there's no "evidence" that you should.* Trust God anyway. His silence and apparent absence is beckoning your spirit to be embraced by His grace. *You'll make it through more than you can ever imagine.*

You're stronger in Him than you could ever fathom. Your times of trials, your times of "waiting," are teaching you to lean longer and harder on God than you ever thought you could. He's growing your faith in ways that you cannot conceive.

Press through the doubt and stand in the pain. Find rest in His Promises and embrace in the dark what He has revealed to you by His Light. When all hope is gone, there is faith . . . and faith brings about God's presence and power. Don't give into despair . . . know that *God is there* and He *does* care. Know that even though He may be silent, *it is in His silence that He is speaking.*

—————∞•❀•∞—————

It's within an instant, suddenly, without notice, that life can take a dramatic turn for the worse. Just when you're certain that you're standing on solid ground, you feel yourself begin to sink, and in utter helplessness, all you can do is cry out to God. The "waiting place" is the place where God *seems* to be silent. You may have "waited" on God in the past and He showed up, but this time He's nowhere to be found. And His silence trumps the burden that's pulling you under. God's silence in desperate times is difficult at best; it can be frustrating and excruciating.

There may have been times in the past when God was directing you, leading you, blessing you, but now it appears that He has simply walked away. In such trying times, when you're unable to sense God's presence and hear His voice, you will feel abandoned, confused, and terribly alone . . . *but you are not.*

In those times where your voice seems to be rebounding off heaven's floor, when you're hoping God will hear you, yet you feel "unheard," when you're expecting God to show up, but He just doesn't, remember these things:

God's Silence is NOT His Absence. All of our Christian life we're prepared to hear God speak to us, *but nothing prepares us for His silence.* When our emotions are flooding our soul and we "feel" the absence of His presence, we can calm and strengthen our frightened hearts with the truth of Psalm 139:7, 9-12 (NIV):

> *Where can I go from your Spirit?*
> *Where can I flee from your presence?*

If I settle on the far side of the sea,
even there your hand will guide me,
your right hand will hold me fast.
If I say, 'Surely the darkness will hide me
and the light become night around me,'
even the darkness will not be dark to you.

God's silence becomes our opportunity to enter into the silence with Him. It is our invitation to shift our relationship from one that demands words . . . to an intimate relationship where *no words are necessary.* We may not be able to "see" God or "feel" Him in our "waiting place," but He is there. The question is, "Do *you* believe He is?"

God's Silence Tests Our Faith. It doesn't take much faith to trust in a Savior who is walking beside you and constantly performing miracles. But what happens when He's crucified on a cross? What happens when it's Saturday? What happens when Sunday just isn't here yet and you're not sure if God is going to fulfill His Promises? We're no different than the Disciples in times of despair, when God was nowhere to be found . . . they ran, they hid, they forgot all that Jesus had told them.

God calls us to trust Him each and every day, in each and every moment, whether we're high upon a mountain top or in the deepest valley. His silence puts our faith to the test. God's silence is proving our faith.

It's like a parent teaching their child to ride a bike. In the beginning, they walk or run beside them; holding on to them, talking them through the process, and preventing them from falling. They're working to build their confidence. But, at some point, the parent lets go. It's not that the parent doesn't care or isn't there, it's that they know they've shown their child how it's done; in their wisdom, they *know it's time for the child to practice what they've been taught.* So, God's silence, at times, is preparing us for the road ahead. He's building our commitment and perseverance. And through the test, those things that we're trusting more than Him will be revealed. He knows that if we're going to journey with Him, we're in for the ride of our life, and we will need to have the faith that . . .

> *"doesn't believe without proof,*
> *but trusts without reservation."*
> —D. Elton Trueblood

God's Silence Doesn't Mean Nothing's Happening.
Know this: Breakthrough can come as a result of God's silence. How? Have you ever tried to watch a seed grow? The truth is you can't. Everything that happens to a seed is underground . . . in the dark soil. Sometimes, there are things in our lives that need to be brought to the surface. What you'll find is that it's in God's silence that His Spirit is working within you to reveal those things that must be dealt with to move you forward in your faith walk. He's growing deep roots that will not only nourish you, but make you strong to withstand the rest of the growth process.

Most of the work that's done revolves around surrender. We want to grow up to be a tulip . . . He's growing a rose. To be grown by God, things must be surrendered . . . mainly our fleshly desires. We must come to a place in our faith where we let go of our will and fully embrace His. God's silence must do its work, and His silence will continue for as long as it takes to accomplish His purposes. But, just as we trust that the dawn always brings light that breaks the night, so too, we can trust that our darkness will come to an end.

God's silence will accomplish more in you than you ever imagined, if you will continue to seek Him.

The "waiting place" is the "perfect place" for God to work without all the distractions. Through His silence you will develop a deeper intimacy with Him, you'll find that He's worth trusting, and you'll discover strength in Him that defies all understanding. In those moments when God's silence is deafening, remind yourself of the Truth that the Disciples forgot when they felt He had abandoned them, (Jesus said:) ***"Be sure of this: I am with you ALWAYS, until the end of time."*** If you're trusting in that promise, then you can be assured that as you "wait" for God . . . *He will never be late.*

⸺⸳∞⸳⸺

While we're in our "waiting place," time is everything. We're watching the clock and God doesn't seem to be paying attention to it at all. What we find, as we agonize over each passing hour, is that God is in no hurry. We are reminded of the truth in 2 Peter 3:8 (NLT): *"But you must not forget this one thing, dear friends: A day is like a thousand years to the Lord, and a thousand years is like a day."* While we're thinking it may very well take God a thousand years to show up in our situation, He knows it will only take Him a day. We're hoping that day will be today, but He knows the whole scope of the plan. And what we don't realize is that we will miss out on God's best in our lives when we do not wait upon His guidance and trust in *His* timing. Trying to rush ahead of God or lagging behind Him will keep us from receiving His greatest blessings. Jesus showed us the greatest example of God's perfect timing when He raised Lazarus from the dead.

Many know this story, but few have looked into the heart of its message. This message is critical to your faith and vital in understanding the ways of God in your "waiting place." We learn from the Bible that Lazarus, Martha, and Mary were dear friends of Jesus. Yet, when the news arrived that Lazarus was sick, Jesus did not rush to him right away. Instead, He declared, *"Lazarus's sickness will not end in death . . .*

No, it is for the glory of God.

I, the son of God, will receive glory from this" (John 11:4). Jesus was giving His followers faith for the moment; many times, God will do the same for us. He gives us only enough information to keep us moving in the right direction. He wants us seeking Him constantly so that we remain in His will—fully dependent upon Him.

As the story continues, Jesus gets word that Lazarus has died. Jesus then tells His followers, "Lazarus is dead. And for your sake, *I am glad I wasn't there, because this will give you another opportunity to believe in me.* Come, let's go see him" (John 11:14).

When Jesus returns to meet Mary and Martha, they're in their "waiting place." They expected Jesus to come, but he hasn't shown up like they thought He would. But, when He finally arrives, they can't help but cry out, "*Lord, if you had been here,* my brother would not have died" (John 11:21).

Many times in life, just like Mary and Martha, we do believe in the power of God, but because He didn't show up when we thought He should . . . we feel like He let us down. In the trials of our lives, in our "waiting places," we're overcome with doubt in our faith because we feel that God could have been there and He wasn't. Quite frankly, we become angry that He just plain didn't show up when we needed Him. As Jesus looked upon those mourning, He too wept. But not tears of sorrow for the death of His friend. Jesus knew Lazarus would be raised from the dead.

Jesus cried not only because of His compassion for those mourning, but because He saw the lack of faith around Him. Jesus knew that without faith, we will miss out on God's very best; He fully understood the importance of trusting God along the way . . . even when we don't have all the answers and uncertainty is our dearest friend.

Jesus concludes this miracle by raising Lazarus from the dead and declaring, *"Didn't I tell you that you would see God's glory if you believe"* (John 11:40)? I can almost hear the voice of Jesus telling each of us now,

> *"Didn't I tell you that you*
> *would see God's glory if you believe?"*

The question you must ask yourself is "Where is my faith lacking?" What situations are you going through that you believe in God and His awesome power, yet there remains a hint of doubt that He might not show up on time? When you trust in God completely and cling to His Word, you will come to understand that **God is never late, and He's usually not early . . . He's always *right on time*.** In your "waiting place," when nothing's happening and you're tempted to doubt, let go of your fears by grabbing hold of your faith and be *expecting* God's perfectly timed arrival.

—oo‿●‿oo—

While we wait on God, our heart still begs the question, "Why?" As our spirit is consumed with hopelessness, we wonder if God is *truly* trustworthy. We may not be able to fully understand God's ways, but He has given us glimpses of how he works throughout the Bible. We find in the book of Exodus that, often times, our lives are no different from the Israelites in the desert—except that we have a much greater understanding of God's ways . . . we can read the Bible and see God's Promises continually fulfilled. We can witness His faithfulness from beginning to end.

In this particular account, God had led His chosen people, slaves, out of captivity. Yet, their behavior showed no gratitude or trust in God. Throughout the plagues of Egypt (Exodus 7:14-12:30), the Israelites saw amazing miracles, and yet, they did not walk forward with the understanding that God was in control. Their behavior certainly did not represent a love of God, when on their way out of Egypt they robbed the Egyptians of gold and silver (see Exodus 12:35-36). Even as they headed toward the Red Sea, out of captivity, as Pharaoh's army closed in, they were furious with Moses. They said to him:

Was it because there were no graves in Egypt
that you brought us to the desert to die?
What have you done to us by bringing us out of Egypt?
Didn't we say to you in Egypt,
'Leave us alone; let us serve the Egyptians?'
It would have been better for us to serve
the Egyptians than to die in the desert!
Exodus 12:11-12 (NIV)

Throughout the Israelites' lives, they failed to see God's provision. God's power was so mightily demonstrated to them when He parted the Red Sea . . . you'd think that *one* miracle would be enough to convince anyone of the power of God for a lifetime! Yet we learn,

In the desert the whole community grumbled against
Moses and Aaron. The Israelites said to them,
'If only we had died by the Lord's hand in Egypt!
There we sat around pots of meat and ate all the food
we wanted, but you have brought us out into this desert
to starve this entire assembly to death.'
Exodus 16:2-3 (NIV)

God heard them and sent quail and manna to eat. He provided enough water to sustain them in a desert. Now, *didn't they just see the parting of the Red Sea . . . on top of all the many other miracles He had already performed?* How could they have so little faith? Even as Moses went up on Mount Sinai, people were still complaining. God's manna wasn't enough, they wanted something better . . . they wanted *more*. They were far from content in their circumstances, and *God's patience* was wearing thin (see Numbers 11:18-20 NLT):

"Now the Lord will give you meat, and you will eat it. You will not eat it for just one day, or two days, or five, ten or twenty days, but for a whole month— until it comes out of your nostrils and you loathe it— because you have rejected the Lord, who is among you, and have wailed before him, saying, 'Why did we ever leave Egypt?'"

And so, God's chosen people continued to complain with very little faith. *They had faith when God showed up*, but the moment the miracle had passed, they were back to self indulgence. It's called living from one spiritual high to the next . . . we're all guilty of it. We don't like our "waiting places." If God can show up whenever He wants to . . . *"Why doesn't He?"*

Why do we have to *wait*?

The Israelites wandered in the desert for forty years because of their lack of faith. It was a trip that should have only taken eleven days! So, as we look at our own lives, as we long for the Promised Land, the land of milk and honey, the place in our lives where we can experience peace and joy, we can find God . . . *in the desert of our lives.* We find Him in our waiting place where we're suffering. Even in the midst of our complaining and lack of faith, ***God is there.***

What we learn from the rest of this account in the Bible is that far from many who began the journey to the Promised Land actually saw it. All of them could have, and would have, *if they would have chosen God, in the way that He had chosen them.* Instead of questioning God and His ways, *they should have been questioning their own.* What we find is that there is purpose in pain. There is a reason that we're "waiting."

You see, when God shows up in our lives, it seems as though He "suddenly" arrived . . . but it's really no surprise . . . it has happened just as He planned all along. The fullness of God's plans is far too difficult for us to even begin to understand. So, this "waiting place" brings us to a place of having to completely rely in and trust in Him . . . even when we cannot see the very next step in front of us. Our faith should always believe that our lives are lived best in the timing of God, not our own. And we should live by the faith we profess. If God says He uses ALL things for good . . .

then we should believe it.

*And we know that God causes **everything**
to work together for the good of those who love God
and are called according to his purpose for them.*
Romans 8:28 (NLT)

If God works all things together for good, then what purpose does our "waiting place" have in our lives? When we have questions for God, He has questions for us too.

And it's in the "waiting place" where He is able to get our attention and draw us near as He reveals our hearts. And mostly what we find is that we're more like the Israelites than we care to admit. In spite of all the Lord has done for us, all the times He has provided and sustained us in our darkest hours, we still complain and doubt Him in every way. It's in our "waiting place" that the heat of the desert reveals:

-our doubt in God
-our fears
-our desire to be in control
-our rebellious nature
-our pride
-our desires that take the place of God
-our lack of trust in God

God knows that as we travel through life in "comfort" mode, we're missing some of the deeper issues hidden within our hearts. We're concerned about fixing our external circumstances—God is more concerned with fixing the internal ones.

In our "waiting place," it's the sin in our lives that God wants to work on. He will keep us in our "waiting place" as long as necessary to complete His purposes in it. And for most of us, God has a lot of work to do . . .

so we may find ourselves in a "waiting place" a while longer than we'd like.

As God exposes our sinful hearts, He also reveals that we are quick to forget the many miracles He has performed in our lives. He shows us how easily we forget His provision and power. God allows us to experience and witness our disbelief in our deepest valleys. He shows us that we so easily take Him for granted. But, He's drawing us nearer with each passing moment. It's in our "waiting place," where we realize that we're not in control . . . **God is.** And the sooner we come to grips with that Truth, the more ready we'll be to move forward with God.

Just like the Israelites, God has chosen us and He has made a way for us . . . *through* the desert. In our "waiting place," God is at work. He has much to accomplish if He is preparing us to live with Him for eternity.

So God led the people around by the desert road . . .
Exodus 13:18 (NIV)

Our "waiting" place is more than what it appears to be on the surface. Through extreme heat, lack of necessities, and endless struggles, God is showing us our desperate need for Him and Him alone. He wants us to remember that it is Him that is leading us . . . *even if it's into a desert*. He wants us trusting that He has purpose in it. And He wants us expecting Him to show up. *"Then Jesus said:*

> *'Did I not tell you that if you believed,*
> *you would see the glory of God?'"*
>
> John 11:40 (NIV)

—◦◦◦◦◦◦◦—

While you wait on God, He wants you to prepare yourself for His answer, by seeking Him and finding contentment in your current circumstances. If you are enjoying your life "as is," then you're demonstrating your faith in Him regardless of what you see. You're showing Him that you are ready to receive what He has for you; you're showing Him you know how to walk by faith. You're telling Him, you'll wait as long as He sees necessary to accomplish His purposes in and through your life.

When you walk by faith, you're showing God gratitude and thanks, declaring your faith in Him, living out your belief that He is sovereign. So, if we're truly trusting God, *if we're believing that He is who He says He is,* if we believe He is sovereign . . . then our Spirit and soul should be content. In Philippians 4:11-12, the Apostle Paul said,

*I have learned to be content in whatever circumstances
I am. I know how to get along with humble means,
and I also know how to live in prosperity;
in **any and every circumstance**.
I have learned the secret of being filled
and going hungry, both of having
abundance and suffering need.*

Here's the secret: It's trusting God . . . it's relying on Him for your every need. It's walking by faith and not by sight. It's contentment that is firmly grounded in Christ.

Listen, waiting on God is never wasted time . . . it doesn't mean doing nothing. God can use the "waiting times" in our lives for greater purposes than we can possibly imagine. Use your "waiting" times to draw nearer to Him and use them to gain strength for what lies ahead. While we wait upon God, He's getting us in step with Him, He's working behind the scenes, and He's preparing us for His answers to our prayers. Trust

God, He won't let you down.

Then you will know that I am the Lord;
those who hope in me will not be disappointed.
Isaiah 49:23 (NIV)

Although it can often times *seem* like time is being wasted, like nothing is happening, and possibly God has forgotten about us . . . we must get the facts straight, so that we do not live a lie . . . we must clearly understand that if we're declaring our faith in God, **He never lets go.** You see, *it's not that God has abandoned us . . . it's that many times, too often, we abandon Him.* In our "waiting place," it's not that God is not there, it's that we don't acknowledge that He is. And as we sit anxiously waiting, we hear the still small voice once again saying, *"Where is your faith?"*

———oo°°°oo———

One of the most critical decisions in your faith that you will continually make throughout your life is, *"Do you trust God, or not?"* Do you believe He's holding on to you or not? It is a question you must answer ... *it is the* decision in your faith that determines the outcome of your life.

Here's a little story, you'll surely enjoy, and hopefully you'll take its message with you in your life:

Some years ago, on a hot summer day in Florida, a little boy decided to go for a swim in the old swimming hole behind his house. In a hurry to dive into the cool water, he ran out the back door, leaving behind shoes, socks, and shirt as he went. He flew into the water, not realizing that as he swam toward the middle of the lake, an alligator was swimming toward the shore.

His mother, in the house, was looking out the window and saw the two as they got closer and closer together. In utter fear, she ran toward the water yelling to her son as loudly as she could. Hearing her voice, the little boy became alarmed and made a U-turn to swim to his mother. It was too late. Just as he reached her, the alligator reached him. From the dock, the mother grabbed her little boy by the arms just as the alligator snatched his legs. That began an incredible tug-of-war between the two. The alligator was much stronger than the mother, but the mother was much too passionate to let go.

A farmer happened to drive by, heard her screams, raced from his truck, took aim and shot the alligator. Remarkably, after weeks and weeks in the hospital, the little boy survived . . . His legs were extremely scarred by the vicious attack of the animal, and on his arms, were deep scratches where his mother's fingernails dug into his flesh in her effort to hang on to the son she loved.

The newspaper reporter who interviewed the boy after the trauma, asked if he could show him his scars. The boy lifted his pant legs. And then, with obvious pride, he said to the reporter,

"But look at my arms.
I have great scars on my arms too.
I have them because my mom wouldn't let go."

We can relate in our lives as we reflect upon God's love for us. The enemy has been pulling on us, tugging on us, and we have scars. We have scars of a painful past . . . of sins that have left their mark. And our greatest sin is our unbelief during our "waiting places." But what we must never forget is that **some of those wounds are because God refused to let go**. In the midst of all that you've been through, God has been holding on to you. In your "waiting place," as you fight through the pain and suffering,

God never lets go.

While you're "waiting" on God in your life, as you're struggling with the difficult circumstances in your life, God wants to increase your faith and draw you near to Him. He wants to reveal Himself to you in greater, unexpected, faith-changing ways and bring you to a place of contentment and peace—knowing that HE is holding on to you, He is in control, and He is overseeing and working in and through every detail of your life.

You may not be able to understand His ways, you may not even get a glimpse of what He's up to, but if you're trusting in His Word, you can know with confident assurance that He is working *all things for good, He is with you always*, and *He will never leave you nor forsake you.* And as you wait, you can find peace through God and know that *Dr. Seuss* had it all *wrong...* the *"waiting place"* is *not* a useless place. In fact, to God, it's the most *"useful" place*:

You'll get so strengthened

that your spirit will soar

up top of mountains where you'll find God once more

you'll travel your journey in peace and find rest

as you trust in your God who always knows best

You'll find true joy in seeing God face to face

And all of it happens in <u>the most useful place</u>...

The Waiting Place...

—Cherie Hill

BONUS FEATURE:

1st Chapter of

BE STILL

Let Jesus Calm Your Storms

Cherie Hill

Praise for *Be Still*

"With this detailed study of the incident of Jesus calming the storm, Cherie Hill has not only brought new light to a familiar Gospel story, she has showed us how to both weather and grow from our personal storms. *Be Still* is a healing balm to the soul. My best advice — get this book, use it, and buy another one for your best friend!"
— Jim Thomson, M.A., LCPC, author and speaker.

"*Be Still* is a wealth of Scripture that readers can return to again and again for encouragement in the midst of trials. *Be Still* is not a book that you read once, put on your bookshelf, and then forget about. It's a book that doesn't promise quick fixes, or endless sunshine. Instead, it is a lifeline attached to God's Word, designed to help the reader find peace in the midst of each and every storm that comes their way."
— Deborah Porter, writer, editor, and radio talk show host.

"*Be Still — Let Jesus Calm Your Storms* combines intellectual common sense, Biblical scriptures, and an author dedicated to helping people who have suffering in their lives. If you are currently going through a storm, this book can definitely help you through it. Buy a copy for yourself, buy a copy for a friend, or leave a copy somewhere for a stranger."
— Dan Blankenship, author of *The Running Girl.*

"The book nicely bridges the gap between those who doubt God because there are storms and the true lessons to be drawn from those storms. One of the best parts of this book is the way the author explores creating both inner and outer peace. Many people are more troubled in their minds than they are in reality; this book can help."
—Donald M. Mitchell, Amazon.com top 10 Reviewer, Harvard Graduate, author, and CEO featured in *Forbes Magazine*.

"*Be Still, Let Jesus Calm Your Storms,* by Cherie Hill, is an inspiring book that Christians, as well as all individuals who are seeking peace in a chaotic world, will find to be 'life-changing.' Regardless of where readers are in their walk with God, the words of the author and her use of Scripture to support her advice and encouragement will enable them to understand much more about faith and how it is the path that gives peace of mind in all situations."
—Bettie Corbin Tucker, Publisher, IP book reviewer, former radio talk show host, and published author.

"I can highly recommend this book to anyone who is looking for a fulfilling life purpose. Cherie Hill has a Bachelor of Arts in Psychology and has a Certificate in Biblical Counseling, but her greatest accomplishment is making a difference in the lives of people who are in need of human caring, a few warm words of encouragement and an open heart."
—Rebecca Johnson, Amazon.com top 10 Reviewer.

BE STILL

Let Jesus Calm Your Storms

Cherie Hill

This book is dedicated to God...

the *perfect author* of my life.

My greatest joy is just in "knowing" You.

Thank you for teaching me to "*Be Still.*"

Most of all, thank you for loving me enough

to use my life according to *Your* purposes.

Contents

Preface

I would like to take a moment to explain exactly how this book was inspired and why I believe it can deeply change your life.

As a born again Christian, I began asking God to give my life purpose and fill me in a way that the world could not. I needed something that was eternal and meaningful. And well, God answered me. I believe that God has always had a plan for me, yet it was only when I finally reached out to Him that He revealed His purpose for my life. God began to show me all of the "spiritual gifts" that He had given to me. He gave me insight as to how all of my life experiences had strengthened and developed those gifts.

You see, I have always been a good listener. For some reason, people have always felt more than comfortable revealing their most intimate problems in their lives to me. I never understood why complete strangers would open up and express their deepest pains and "storms" of life, while looking to me for some type of answer. Many times, I found myself overwhelmed with empathy, yet filled with sorrow because I was unable to provide answers or even point them in the right direction. When God finally revealed His plan for my life, I began to see the whole picture come together. God had a vision for my life…and it was in my moment of surrender that He gave me eyes to see.

God began to teach me how critical Scripture is to our

lives; His Word has become the very breath that gives me life. His plan for me was to lead others to Jesus by simply providing them with Scriptures that would speak directly to their circumstances. It is in receiving God's grace that we can live with confident hope – it is His Word that gives us the faith we need to receive that grace. It really is the Truth that sets us free and fills us with hope. His Word produces a faith in us that will never fail.

And so, to make a long story short, God revealed "ScriptureNow.com" to me. I can honestly tell you that it has been the greatest blessing in my life and in the lives of hundreds of thousands of people in over 30 countries around the world. I can't imagine one day of my life going by without reaching out and sharing the Word of God to people in this way! And God did all of this in the midst of my raging storms of life.

This is where "Be Still" took on its purpose...as I have read the countless prayer requests through ScriptureNow.com, God spoke to me and showed me the miracle of "Jesus Calms the Storm" in a whole new light. This miracle goes to the heart of every single situation that we face in life, and I believe God filled me with the wisdom and insight to be able to write this book for you.

*I hope that this book touches your heart and speaks to you through its message. I pray that you will always draw close to God, so that He can comfort, encourage, and rescue you through all of life's storms. I pray that you will also visit me at: **http://www.ScriptureNow.com** and experience a great blessing in your life!*

Testimonies from ScriptureNow.com

Oh, what a blessing...I am so thankful to God that I found your website. God speaks to me through you.

Thank you for your Scriptures, they seem to always come on time.

Thank you! It's amazing how the Scriptures have gone in line with what I am dealing with!!

Thank you so much for your never ending help in my life. The Scriptures were helpful, powerful, and effective in my life.

You have helped save my life. My crisis is over and God gave me a miracle!

God bless you mightily for your compassionate ministry.

I don't know how you knew, but this Scripture was exactly what I needed. Thank you!!!

Thank you. This is what I needed to hear!

Thank you for all of your prayers and love over this year and for being a safe place to call out to. I can't tell you just how much the daily Scriptures have blessed my heart.

You know, before I found out about ScriptureNow.com, I was not lost, but not headed in the right direction.

I will never be able to express the power I have experienced in the Scriptures that you send.

You will never fully understand how God has used your website to turn my life around and get me moving in the right direction.

I had lost all hope until I found your website, and now I am filled with a hope I have never felt before.

The nine Scriptures that you sent have given me nine days of strength. I had never experienced God speaking to me until now. Thank you for using His Word to help me hear Him.

I look so forward to receiving your Daily Scripture. It just seems as though God is speaking right through it!

You will never quite understand the impact your Ministry is having.

Thank you from the bottom of my heart for your prayers and your concerns. I don't think I could have coped with the pressures I have found myself under if it would not have been for your caring and sending me Scripture and prayer. I now know that I will overcome through Christ!

May God richly bless you for the work you are doing for Him.

I'm wondering if this is really God's email...the Scriptures you send speak so directly to me...that it must be.

Introduction

The Storm

Do you feel as though you're in a raging storm? Storms of life flood your spirit with disillusionment, despair, and disappointment. The consuming waves of a storm in life can submerge your soul with agonizing fear. When you're in a storm of life, it feels as though each breath might be your last. The ongoing destruction from the storm forces you to cling to anything and everything, in the hopes of somehow surviving it all. As the storm continues to rage, you suddenly realize that there's no lifeboat — there's no quick escape. You're on your own. Usually, very quickly, the terror sets in; with it comes despair and hopelessness. The desperation that overcomes you, suddenly, becomes more than you can withstand. As the end seems to be drawing nearer, with each moment that passes, all you can do is stand by and watch it all unfold.

Our storms of life bring us to the point where we realize that we have nowhere to go, but to God. In a moment of overwhelming desperation, when we finally do call out to Him, we suddenly realize that our relationship with Him has grown cold. Through our cries for help, without stable ground to stand on, it's anger that takes over and we shout, *"Lord, don't you care?"*

We've all been there, at one time or another. If you haven't experienced a storm in your life, then praise God; but, get ready because Jesus assured us:

I have told you all this so that you may have peace in me.
Here on earth you will have many trials and sorrows.
But take heart, because I have overcome the world.
(John 16:33 NLT)

The Controversy of the Miracle

The miracle of "Jesus Calms the Storm" has been called one of the most controversial miracles that Jesus performed. Even today, we witness those who are pronounced dead…receive life again, blind who against all odds see, illnesses that are cured without explanation, and tragic accidents where miraculously people survive. We witness miracles every day and realize that they are from the power of something far greater than what we can comprehend.

Yet, even in the face of such miracles, we allow human reasoning to get the best of us. Doubt, more often than not, wins out. We end up walking by sight, instead of by faith. So, we wrestle with our faith, just as the Disciples did on the Sea of Galilee.

The battle begins...*within*. How do we accept someone controlling the wind and the waves in a violent storm? Even if we want to believe, this kind of miracle pushes our faith a little farther than we'd like. This kind of faith presses us beyond our comfort zone.

We like to keep God in a box. We're comfortable with Him in some things in our lives, but not others. We're content in keeping Him where we've put Him...allowing Him out of the box is just too risky—we're not sure what to expect from Him. We're not convinced He'll do things the *way* they should be done or in the *timing* that they should be done. We believe that it's possible for Him to heal someone we're praying for, but we're just not certain that He can do anything in *our* situation. We're convinced that there are just some things that God is either too busy to deal with, or He just really doesn't care. It has been said that to ask God for help in "small things" is wasting His time—be assured, *ALL things are small to God.* He is looking to and fro the earth for someone to not only call out to Him, but to *believe Him* (2 Chronicles 16:9).

He is looking for *your* faith *in the midst of your storms of life*. He has allowed the storm, in an effort to increase your faith, *by threatening to destroy it.* Out of His great love for you, He calls out to you through your storm and asks, *"Who do you say I am"*

(Matthew 16:15)? As your life is pushed to the edge, His voice calls down from heaven . . . demanding an answer.

It is your answer that determines whether or not you will make it through the storm and if there will be anything left in the aftermath. It is your faith in God that makes *all* the difference. Trust Him, and cling to your faith...God ALWAYS keeps His Word.

According to your faith
and trust and reliance
[on the power invested in Me]
be it done to you;
(Matthew 9:29 AMP)

This miracle is for you to understand
the purpose of the storms in your life
and how to persevere through them.
By applying this miracle to your life,
you will find that God can calm
all of your storms . . .
if you will just have faith that He can.

The miracle in the storm on the Sea of Galilee revealed the Disciples' lack of faith in Jesus as the

Son of God. Although they had witnessed Jesus perform many miracles, they still had doubt about who He really was. It was through this miracle that their faith was truly put to the test. The Disciples believed, just as most people did, that many miracles are understandably possible, *but only God* could control the wind and the waves. There was no doubt in their minds that this kind of power could only come from the hand of God. God's desire is to move His hand in your storms, as well. *He is looking for your faith.*

What you must understand is that this miracle was not just a story of God's awesome power—it was not just another miracle. This miracle was for you to understand the purpose of the storms in *your* life and how to persevere through them. By applying this miracle to your life, you will find that God can calm all of your storms…*if you will just have faith that He can.*

Storms Will Come

After receiving thousands of emails from people all over the world through the ScriptureNow.com Ministry, I might guess that your storms are a broken relationship, a shattered marriage, depression, despair over unsaved loved ones, job anxiety, unemployment, financial failure, an illness, death, or some unexpected tragedy. Maybe you feel that life in general is a raging storm. No matter how big or small your storm, you feel that no one seems to understand; you're convinced that you're in the boat alone. With each agonizing moment that passes, you feel that you're one day closer to drowning; it seems as though nothing and no one can save you.

If you aren't currently in a storm, be on the lookout. The enemy is looking for an opportunity to send the perfect storm into your life. He is well aware of our deepest desires and our innermost struggles. Satan not only attacks us where we are weakest; more often, he attacks in those areas where we feel we are strongest. He knows exactly where pride exists. He knows we won't see an attack coming when we're overly confident in a particular area of our lives. He knows those places in our lives where we've decided to play God and we've shut God out. He's able to see any crack we leave in the doorway, and He feels more than comfortable letting himself in. The enemy is always at work, and he is more than willing to kick you while you're down. He's not particularly concerned about what's going on in your life and whether or not the timing is convenient. He's simply out to destroy your faith in God. The enemy's attacks are deceitful and destructive—you won't even see what's coming. Just as in the miracle of Jesus Calms the Storm, many times, the storms of our lives will come from out of nowhere — *unexpectedly*.

Faith isn't faith, unless it believes in the unseen. It doesn't take faith at all to cling to what you see. Faith in God trusts Him even when you can't see the very next step in front of you.

How many times have we judged others and said, "I'd never do that. That could never happen to me...I'm too loving, too giving, too faithful, too loyal, too obedient, too prayerful, too dedicated to God. Besides, I go to church on Sunday!" Before we know it, we find ourselves in the midst of that *very* storm; we're dazed and confused, wondering how we got there and how to get out.

The Storm Has Great Purpose

The Disciples were not exempt from a test of faith and neither are we. God's purposes for them were so great, so critical to His plans, that He allowed a raging storm to take over their boat on the Sea of Galilee — bringing them to the edge of their faith. He increased their faith by asking them to step into a boat and *risk it*.

Faith isn't faith, unless it requires taking a step into the unseen. It doesn't take faith at all to cling to what you see. The faith that God is after is a faith that clings to Him and isn't threatened or destroyed by adversity and uncertainty. You know that you have genuine faith when common sense tells you to stop believing, but you continue to trust God anyway. *It's all about your faith in God*—don't ever believe otherwise.

This unexpected storm tested these men, who considered themselves *very* skilled fishermen, so that their faith would be strengthened for the journey ahead. In their weakness, they realized they were helpless without their Savior. When Jesus performed the incredible miracle of calming the storm, it caused these expert fishermen, who had been through many storms on this Sea, to experience a storm that would bring them to the end of themselves. Although the Disciples were master fishermen, God took the area of the Disciples' lives where they felt most confident...and tested them. God knew they needed to be brought to the end of their own abilities, so that they would trust in His.

Rest assured, God is bringing you to your knees, so that you can witness His hand lift you up. The message that God needed the Disciples to understand was that it was *by faith alone* that they could be saved. It's the message He wants *you* to know, as well.

But people are declared righteous
because of their faith,
not because of their work.
(Romans 4:5 NLT)

By sending the storm and testing them in it, God turned these men into the greatest witnesses for Christ that the world has ever known. Our storms will also come in those areas where we least expect them.

Don't be deceived,
God has allowed the storm in your life...
with a plan to use it ALL
for your good and HIS glory!

Our pride will keep us from seeing the storms coming. It is in the areas where pride exists that Satan sees an easy target. Don't be deceived...God *allowed* the storm in this miracle, and He's allowing it in your life...with a plan to use it ALL for *your good* and His glory!

Then the Lord asked Satan, 'Have you noticed my servant Job? He is the finest man in all the earth – a man of complete integrity. He fears God and will have nothing to do with evil.' Satan replied to the Lord, 'Yes, Job fears

God, but not without good reason! You have always pro-
tected him and his home and his property from harm. You
have made him prosperous in everything he does. Look
how rich he is! But take away everything he has, and he
will surely curse you to your face!' 'Alright, you may test
him,' the Lord said to Satan. 'Do whatever you want with
everything he possesses, but don't harm him physically.'
So Satan left the Lord's presence.
(Job 1:8-12 NLT)

Never doubt that there are spiritual conversations about *you*. Yes, *you*! You are known by name in the heavenly realms, and we know this from Isaiah 45:3 (NLT):

> *I am the Lord, the God of Israel,*
> *the one who calls you by name.*

You are no different than Job or the Disciples, in that, God will only allow those things which He knows will bring you closer to Him, give Him the glory, and make your heart more like His. It is im-perative to truly understand that God will never give you more than you can withstand, and He will always make a way through your storms when you trust in Him.

> *But remember that the temptations that come into*
> *your life are no different from what others experience.*
> *And God is faithful. He will keep the temptation from*

becoming so strong that you can't stand up against it.
When you are tempted, he will show you a
way out so that you will not give into it.
(1 Corinthians 10:13 NLT)

When you feel that God has allowed your storms, you should be comforted in just knowing that God alone is control of them. In your storms of life, your spirit can be quieted by grabbing hold of the Truth: If God has allowed a storm . . . *He will make a way through it.*

If God has allowed the storm,
He will make a way through it.
Be certain that God is only allowing the storm
because He knows the blessing behind it.
Through the storm, God is giving
you the opportunity to experience,
first hand, His miraculous and sufficient
power in your life.

He has assured you that He is with you *always* (Matthew 28:20). You should feel secure, in just knowing, that God has set the boundaries and perimeters of your storm—just as he did with Job. It should strengthen you to know that God is allowing this storm only because He knows the blessing behind it.

When God is at work in your life, you will often experience the miraculous and sufficient power of God in your storms . . . *even more than in your times of great blessings.* We can only truly appreciate the glory of being on the mountaintop when we've had to climb up from the valley. And the only way from one mountaintop to the next is *through* the valleys. It's in the valley where the richest soil in the world is found...*God knows what He's doing when He's growing your faith.*

It is only through the storms that you will truly know the heart of God. In your storms, you've been given the opportunity to encounter God — the choice to accept His invitation is yours.

As long as we insist on being in control, God will not interfere. He will allow us to go our own way, until we come to a place of surrender. In order to experience God's miracles in our lives, we must be willing to relinquish control, and *let God be God.*

Too often, instead of trusting in God's sovereign purpose in our storms, many of us feel anger. We feel like God allowed us to walk into the storm or that He even led us right into it. We're convinced that He could have spared us the pain and suffering. Understanding the purpose of your storms will help you persevere through them and bring you closer to God, instead of casting your soul deeper into despair by allowing your heart to become hardened in your distress.

In all this, Job did not sin by blaming God.
(Job 1:22 NLT)

(If you have not read the book of Job...I challenge you to do so and understand what it truly means to have faith in God through the most tragic storms of life.)

Why A Storm?

We live in a world filled with anxiety and tremendous uncertainty. Each and every day we are confronted by stories that shake the foundation of our faith—to a point of near destruction. If we, personally, aren't facing unthinkable trials and tragedies, we worry about friends and family members who are facing the inconceivable. Or we become fearful of what *lies ahead* in our lives.

Jesus performs many miracles
in our storms of life—
showing us that He is ALL we need,
when there is a need, is just one of them.

We wonder what *good* could possibly come from such overwhelming anxiety and fear. But, it's in the worst of times that we find the most opportune moment to re-examine our lives. What have we taken for granted? What are our morals and values? On what have we built our foundation and will it be able to withstand the storms in our lives? In the storms of life, we have two choices: we can reaffirm the faith we embraced when we accepted Christ into our life, or we can walk away.

For those who have never known Jesus, these times of suffering are an opportunity for the heart to be opened and the need for God to surface. God is at work, even when we are unaware. The storms convince us that we're lost and in need of help. In our desperation, we realize that we need a "compass."

When you're holding a compass, you can turn your feet in any direction, but the arrow of the compass will faithfully point to Magnetic North. If you should ever become lost, the compass will give you an indication of where you are and where you're going. In life, "North" is Christ. We may take a path that leads us in the "world's" direction and we might get lost along the way; but, when we turn to Christ, He realigns our lives in the direction of God's will. Jesus performs many miracles in our storms of life—showing us that He is all that we need, when there is a need, is just one of them.

Whether you're a person of faith in God, or a person still questioning and seeking answers, it's likely that you're open–minded to miracles. If you don't need a miracle right now, you probably know someone who does. You see, God does extraordinary things for ordinary people. He loves to surprise us with His goodness and His power, in order to help us in our most desperate times. He can do anything. But, in the storms of your life, He wants you to know His presence, so that as you wait for His perfect timing, you can be filled with hope. He wants you to find security and peace in His care; He wants you trusting that He is mighty to save (Zephaniah 3:17).

If you want to find an extraordinary miracle in the life of an ordinary man, you need to look no further than to Moses. Moses was traveling in the desert when God spoke to him through a burning bush. (If you want to get an amazing glimpse of God's awesome power, you should make it a priority to read through the book of Exodus.) God caught Moses off-guard, in the middle of the desert, through a burning bush. His encounter with God was life–altering. This miracle enabled Moses to walk forward in faith, trusting God, because he could not deny such a supernatural occurrence. Moses was able to walk through even greater adversity along his journey because with each step of faith that he took...God strengthened his faith through one miracle after another.

Our storms come with an objective that is far more significant than our present need for comfort. God is doing us a favor, by bringing us to a place of forfeiting our will in our lives, so that we will embrace His.

God used a burning bush to initially get Moses' *attention*; then, when Moses came to examine the bush further, *God called out his name.* (In our storms of life...God calls out our name, too. He wants our undivided attention.) As Moses drew even closer to God, God stopped him and told him to take off his shoes because he was standing on holy ground. He wanted Moses to know that he was in the presence of Almighty God. He wanted him to remember that moment *forever*. That event is now remembered thousands of years later—God's miracle made its mark on history.

In this particular miracle, God didn't stop with a burning bush. He goes on to tell Moses that

He has heard the cries of His people in their suffer ing, and He has come down to save them. In your storms of life, God wants to step in and give you a miracle, too. But, it's less about the actual miracle and more about your encounter with Him. He wants to give you the faith that will see you through the storms of your life that are yet to come. *And they will come.*

The poet Elizabeth Barrett Browning once, famously, wrote that *"Earth is crammed full of heaven, and every common bush aglow with God. Those who see…take off their shoes."* God wants to bring *you* to a place of "taking off *your* shoes."

This miracle on the Sea of Galilee, this storm, was preparing the Disciples' faith for the journey ahead.

It was the storm that would bring them to their knees and really get their attention. God also knows exactly what storms you and I will need to go through, in order to draw us closer to Him. Our storms come with an objective that is far more significant than our present need for comfort. God is doing us a favor by bringing us to a place of forfeiting all of our expectations in our lives, so that we will embrace His. Your storms can create the greatest intimacy between yourself and God. There is *nothing* more awesome. When you're walking with God, the emptiness and loneliness that daily consumes your soul is filled with a joy that overflows and a peace that is beyond all understanding.

Rest assured that God can perform
miracles in your life,
in your storms,
just as He did when He calmed the Sea of Galilee.
The question is,
"Do YOU believe He can?"

This miracle was not just for the Disciples—it was for *you*. You will experience a miracle in your life, if you will understand how significant the storms of your life are to your faith. You must realize that God can do ANYTHING—He *can* calm the storm. But, what He really wants to do is use your life for His purposes—something far greater than anything you could dare ask for or imagine (Ephesians 3:20). He wants to give you something far more fulfilling than you could ever desire.

It should be encouraging to know that if God could take these few ordinary men and use this storm to change the world forever through their testimony…

He can use your storms for His glory, too.

> *God is strengthening our faith*
> *in the storms of our lives,*
> *and He wants us to get*
> *the message loud and clear —*
> *our faith is not strengthened by striving after it,*
> *but by resting in Him, the Faithful One.*

Yes, God wants to use *you*. Rest assured He can perform miracles in your life, in your storms, just as He did when He calmed the Sea of Galilee. The question is, "Do *you* believe He can?"

> *Then Jesus told him,*
> *"You believe because you have seen me.*
> *Blessed are those who haven't seen me*
> *and believe anyway"*
> (John 20:29 NLT).

"What do you mean, 'If I can'?" Jesus asked. "Anything is possible if a person believes" (Mark 9:23 NLT).

God intends to perform a miracle in your life and not have you say, "*How did He do that?*" Instead, He wants for you to have the same experience as the Disciples of Jesus had — it was in their awe and amazement that they asked, "*Who is this man, that even the winds and waves obey him?*"

And they were filled with awe amazement. They said to one another 'Who is this man, that even the winds and waves obey him?' (Luke 8:25 NLT)

God desires for you to be in such awe and amazement of His power that you are less concerned about how He did it, but rather, *who* it is that did it! We beg and beg for miracles in our lives, constantly wondering why God won't do something; yet, when He does, He mystifies us even more. It's our heart He's after, and He's more than willing to bring about a miracle in your life in order to capture it. His miracle for you is that you will not be overcome by your storms, but that you will know Who to come to when your storms emerge. He's strengthening your faith in Him *through* the storms. He wants us to get the message loud and clear: Our faith is not strengthened by striving after it, but by resting in Him, *the Faithful One.*

God knows what He's doing.
Let the storms come, and let the waters rise—
God is taking you deeper

Just as in the Sea of Galilee, God knows our storms often come from out of nowhere. He's well aware that when they do…we're likely to go into shear panic. His miracle for you, in the storm, is that you can be at rest with Him through your faith.

We look at the storms of our lives and too often, ask, *"If God is so loving, why does He allow pain and suffering in my life? What have I done to deserve being a victim in this circumstance? Why do I need to go through this storm? Why can't He just take me around it? I want out and NOW!"* The truth is, God knows us...He knows what it will take to bring us to our knees. It is upon our knees where we learn to walk by faith and receive the peace that only He can provide when storms arise. Remember this clearly: ANYTHING that drops us to our knees and brings us to the foot of the Cross is GOOD for us. In our moments of complete brokenness, when the flesh is weak, but the spirit is willing (Matthew 26:41), He wants us to know: *In Jesus* we will find confident patience, strength, endurance, and peace.

God knows exactly what we need, in order to make it through this journey of life. At times, our journey will take us into unfamiliar, intimidating, territory...which may be exactly where God wants us, so that He can perform His greatest work in our lives.

If we go back to the book of Exodus, and the life of Moses, we find that when Pharaoh finally let the people go, God did not choose to lead them along the main road that ran through the territory — *even though that was the shortest route to the Promised Land.* Here's what He said, *'If the people are faced with a battle, they might change their minds and return to Egypt.' So God led them in a round-about way through the wilderness toward the Red Sea.* (Exodus 13:17-18 NLT) You see, God may have led them the long way, but He was preparing an even greater miracle than Him *rescuing* them.

You might be tempted to believe that God doesn't know what He's doing—that He's causing you to endure unnecessary pain and suffering. But, rest assured, God knows exactly what He's doing. Let the storms come, and let the waters rise—*God is taking you deeper.*

God knows that this won't be the last storm you will encounter in your life. It's a fallen world; He wants to build your faith in Him, so when the sea rages and the storm clouds begin closing in…you will find peace in Him.

Don't worry about anything; instead pray about everything. Tell God what you need, and thank him for all he has done. If you do this, you will experience God's peace, which is far more wonderful than the human mind can understand. His peace will guard your hearts and minds as you live in Christ Jesus.
(Philippians 4:6-7 NLT)

Faith Can Calm the Storm

Through God's Word, we are assured that He can calm the "external" storm; but, the storm He really wants to calm is the one *inside* of you—the "internal" storm. Ask yourself, while reading through this miracle, "Was Jesus just simply telling the wind and the waves, *'Peace! Be Still!'*? Or was there a deeper message?" Jesus was speaking to YOU in this miracle. You see, it took no effort at all for Jesus to calm the external, physical, storm. It was much more important for Him to teach us how to calm the storm within us—the "spiritual" storm.

God wants you in the back of the boat with Jesus —
a place of peace and rest.
He wants you to "Be Still";
yet, we find that "being still" requires action…
it demands your faith.

When you learn how to calm the storm within, through your faith in God, the wind and the waves may be threatening to take you under, but you will find yourself in the eye of the storm…*at peace.*

We can look at a hurricane as being symbolic to our storms of life. Hurricanes have a distinctive feature called an "eye." The eye of a hurricane is in the middle of the spiral of the storm. The eye is produced by the spiraling action of the storm, and it is the area where the air is slowly sinking. When the eye of a hurricane passes over an area, the winds decrease to a gentle breeze and the rain stops. In the eye of the hurricane, you may even be able to see the sun during the day or the stars out at night. Then, as the rest of the storm passes and the wind suddenly changes directions, the storm becomes ferocious again.

God wants you to be in the eye of your storms in life. In the eye, He knows that you will be able to see the light of day and enjoy the beauty of the stars at night. In the eye of storm, the winds and waters may rage around you, but you will be experiencing peace in the midst of it. God has given us His Word, the Scriptures, to keep us from being overcome by the most powerful winds that reside just outside the eye wall of the storm.

Understanding the miracle of "Jesus Calms the Storm" makes us certain of one thing: Whatever the storm is, however fierce, and however the storm came about, God can calm it. The question is, "Will *you* have faith that God can calm *your* storm?" The lesson in this fantastic miracle of "*Jesus Calms the Storm*" is to have confident faith in God and get to the back of the boat with Jesus — a place of peace and rest. What we also learn through this miracle is that "*Being Still,*" actually, requires action. Let the miracle of Jesus calming the storm increase your faith and bring about a miracle in *your life,* by teaching you to "*Be Still.*"

NOTE TO READER: *I encourage you to go through this book and highlight the Scriptures. When you only have a moment, skim through the book and be encouraged!*

*Also, don't miss the section in the back of this book, "**God's Word On...**" Use the section as a reference to God's Promises that will encourage your faith through all your storms of life.*

Chapter 1

⚓ Understanding the Storm ⚓

Jesus Calms the Storm

On that day, when evening had come, he said to them, "Let us go across to the other side." And leaving the crowd, they took him with them in the boat, just as he was. And other boats were with him. And a great windstorm arose, and the waves were breaking into the boat, so that the boat was already filling. But he was in the stern, asleep on the cushion. And they woke him and said to him, "Teacher, do you not care that we are perishing?" And he awoke and rebuked the wind and said to the sea, "Peace! Be Still!" And the wind ceased, and there was a great calm. He said to them, "Why are you so afraid? Have you still no faith? (Mark 4:35-40 ESV)

Then Jesus asked, "Where is your faith?" And they were filled with awe and amazement. They said to one another, "Who is this man, that even the winds and waves obey him?" (Luke 8:25 NLT)

In order to understand the miracle of "Jesus Calms the Storm," we must first understand the power of the sea; what its power represented then and now. According to the Gospels, Jesus' ministry was centered around the Sea of Galilee. While many important events occurred in Jerusalem, Jesus spent most of His ministry along the shore of this freshwater lake. It was there that Jesus gave more than half of His parables and where He performed most of His miracles.

The Sea of Galilee was known for its sudden, violent storms. When it raged, the threat of drowning among fisherman was all too real. The Sea of Galilee is unique in that it is seven hundred feet below sea level, making it the lowest freshwater lake on the earth. At its widest point, the lake measures thirteen miles from north to south and seven and a half miles from east to west. Its deepest point is estimated at around two hundred feet.

The Sea's location was significant because it made the Sea susceptible to the sudden and violent storms. The storms would often develop when an east wind dropped cool air over the warm air rising from the Sea. This change produced well known furious storms, without warning.

Never forget that God is in control.
The question is, "When a storm arises,
will you cry out to the only
One who can help you?"

The word "sea," in Hebrew, comes from the name of the evil god in the Babylonian creation story. It meant "evil" and "a mysterious and threatening force opposed to God." When Hebrews wanted to declare God's authority, they spoke of His power over the sea. In Psalms 89:9 (NKJV), the Psalmist said,

You rule the raging of the sea,

when its waves rise, you still them.

In Psalm 107:23-30 (NLT), we not only find a prophecy of "Jesus Calms the Storm," but an acknowledgement of God's power over the storms.

Some went off in ships, plying the trade routes of the world. They too, observed the Lord's power in action, his impressive works on the deepest seas. He spoke, and the winds rose, stirring up the waves. Their ships were tossed to the heavens and sank again to the depths; the sailors cringed in terror. They reeled and staggered like drunkards and were at wits' end. "Lord, help!" they cried in their trouble, and he saved them from their distress. He calmed the storm to a whisper and stilled the waves. What a blessing was that stillness as he brought them safely into the harbor!

As powerful as storms were and still are today, God is acknowledged to have power over them all. Never forget this truth in your own life: *God is in control.* The question is, "When a storm arises, will you cry out to the *One* who can help you?"

It was known that storms on this Sea could arise from nowhere; so, since Jesus was the Son of God, one might think that *surely* He knew there would be a great storm on this venture across the Sea. And if this were so, why did He choose to take His Disciples into it? You would almost expect, since Jesus was with the Disciples on this trip across the Sea, they would be free from worry. We can be certain they didn't expect to encounter a raging storm that they may have experienced on many other trips.

Certainly, the Disciples who gave up everything in life and obediently followed Jesus would be protected from harm's way. They might even expect that this would be the most wonderful venture across the Sea that they had ever experienced. They more than likely found confidence in their commitment to Jesus and felt secure in His ability to protect them. They loved Jesus, believed in Him, and left behind everything in life to follow Him; yet, the Disciples' devotion did nothing to protect them from the terror of this storm.

In the Boat

Many times, we as Christians feel the same way the Disciples did...when we become a Christian and accept Jesus as Lord and Savior, shouldn't we be protected? We, understandably, *assume* that life should be "easier"; we feel certain that we should instantly have a closer relationship with God. We can falsely believe that we no longer have to endure "storms" in our lives. But, then, suddenly, one day, in one moment in time, we're faced with the painful truth — *it's not the way it works.* Our false expectations can create a storm in and of itself. When life doesn't happen just as we think it should, the winds start roaring and the storm clouds look ferocious. Our faith can begin to fail amidst the overwhelming atmosphere of doubt and despair.

When we make a stand in our faith, when we decide to get into the boat with Jesus, Satan unleashes his rage against us. We are now "officially" his enemy, and the true battle has begun. Shockingly, as we take each step of faith, our storms seem to actually come *more often* than *before* we believed!

When we're faced with the storms that we must endure, when walking with God, we find ourselves in the midst of our storm crying out, *"Why is this happening to me? If You're a God of love, why all this pain? Why do the innocent suffer? If You're a God of or-*

der, why all the chaos? If You're so powerful, why do You seem so incapable? By the way, where are You?" It is at this time that we need to be reminded of the Truth: Jesus told us in John 16:33 (NLT):

> *I have told you all this*
> *so that you may have peace in me.*
> *Here on earth you will have*
> *many trials and sorrows.*
> *But take heart,*
> *because I have overcome the world.*

When you're in the boat with Jesus, the answers to your questions come in many *unexpected* ways. *Sometimes,* they come by way of a storm that threatens to take you under. You see, instead of presenting just an "ordinary" trial with an "ordinary storm," the storm in this miracle would be like no other. This storm would threaten to take the Disciples' very lives. This storm would ultimately test their faith. This miracle would cause the Disciples to ask, *"Who is this man?"*

Jesus didn't come to get you out of the storms in your life—He came to take you through them.

It's interesting that the most violent storm these fishermen had ever experienced was when Jesus, the Son of God, was in the boat with them. It should be comforting to know that in the most violent storms of your life...*Jesus is in the boat with you, too.*

Understanding the storms of your life is realizing that although the waves may start crashing in on you...*Jesus is with you.* More importantly, you must be assured through His Word: He will not allow you to perish, if you will acknowledge His presence in your life and call out His name. Surely, your boat cannot go down with the Son of God in it! Don't be deceived, Jesus didn't come to get you out of the storms in your life—He came to take you *through* them.

In the storms of your life,
God is always at work—
drawing you closer to Him and weaving
all of your paths into His purposes.

You see, God knew that the Disciples needed to go from "here" to "there," in order to experience the miracle. He needed to take them from "here" to "there" in their faith—it's no different in our own lives. God wants to take us from "here," in our faith, and bring us "there" —a place of walking in greater faith for the journey ahead. When you take a journey with Jesus, it's like nothing you've ever experienced. It's simply not of this world. When you're walking with Jesus, you're taking a supernatural, spiritual, journey where He prepares you to live eternally.

Although we may not particularly like some of the paths on our journey…the destination of a closer relationship with God is worth all the storms we may have to endure. If you're following Jesus, you know where you're going — He's assured you of the destination. It's all about the journey getting there. He'll take you step by step because *He doesn't want you to miss a thing.*

I have refined you but not in the way silver is refined.
Rather, I have refined you in the furnace of suffering.
I will rescue you for my sake-yes, for my own sake!
(Isaiah 48:10 NLT)

It is often asked, "Was this the miracle of God calming the storm in the Sea or the miracle of Jesus teaching us how to calm the storm inside of us?" Jesus knew His Disciples' hearts, just like He knows your heart and mine.

O Lord, you have examined my heart and know everything about me. You know when I sit down or stand up. You know my every thought when far away. You chart

the path ahead of me and tell me where to stop and rest.
Every moment you know where I am.
You know what I am going to say even before I say it, Lord.
You both precede and follow me.
You place your hand of blessing on my head.
(Psalm 139:2 NLT)

As God lovingly allows us to venture into the storms of our lives, He is always at work — drawing us closer and closer to Him while weaving all our paths into His purposes. If you're trusting in God, you can't just look at your circumstances and think that is all there is to it. They are a parallel to something deeper and more important concerning the spirit within you.

In the storms of our lives, God will show us that we have a deeper need. We need to develop the faith that glorifies Him. We must recognize that we are in the hands of a loving Father who has put us right where we need to be, in order to teach us His ways and His will.

The answers for the storms in our lives come through the still small voice of God saying, *"I will not let you go down. You have no reason to despair. Rest in My Word. I am with you always."* Through His Word, He assures us that He has everything under control, and there is no reason to fear. In the words of an old Hymn,

Day by day and with each passing moment,
Strength I find to meet my trials here;
Trusting in my Father's wise bestowment,
I've no cause for worry or for fear.

If we want to understand God's purpose in the storm, we must learn that God has allowed the storms in our lives out of love and wisdom. God designed life to be full of the unexpected, so that we will constantly be reminded that *we're not in control.*

Satan fills us with the lies that we are our own gods, we are in charge, we can plan, and we can direct our future; to the degree that God has given us free will…there is some truth to that. But, the devil distorts it and leads us to believe that we can control *everything.* As hard as we might try…*we can't.* Jesus himself reminded us:

I tell you the truth, the Son can do nothing by himself;
(John 5:19 NIV)

Before Jesus' crucifixion, Pilate asked Jesus, *"Don't you realize I have the power either to free you or to crucify you?"* Jesus' answer was simple, revealing, and full of Truth…*"You would have no power over me if it were not given to you from above"* (John 19:11 NIV).

Regardless of what storm we're facing in life, we can never forget the simple truth: *God is in charge.* As difficult as it is for us to understand, God's will in our lives has far greater purposes than we can imagine; yet, all of them are designed for greater good. We must face the Truth that says God is *ultimately* in control.

In understanding God's ways, we cannot decide to heartily accept some Truths, yet readily discount others. We must accept God's ways and trust in them; it's a decision we make that isn't based upon our desires or emotions. We walk by faith in our loving God. Take a moment to really grasp the following truth in Romans 9: 15-19 (NIV):

For he says to Moses, "I will have mercy on whom I have mercy, and I will have compassion on whom I have compassion." It does not, therefore, depend on man's desire or effort, but on God's mercy. For the Scripture says to Pharaoh: "I raised you up for this very purpose, that I might display my power in you and that my name might be proclaimed in all the earth." Therefore God has mercy on whom he wants to have mercy, and he hardens whom he wants to harden. One of you will say to me: "Then why does God still blame us? For who resists his will?" But who are you, O man, to talk back to God? "Shall what is formed say to him who formed it, 'Why did you make me like this?' "Does not the potter have the right to make out of the same lump of clay some pottery for noble purposes and some for common use?"

Even though our storms may come filled with pain and suffering, we are to clearly understand that they come from a loving God...and we must praise Him...*in* the storm.

Should we accept only good things from the hand of God and never anything bad? (Job 2:10 NLT)

An unknown poet expressed the depths of God's work in and through us in this way:

When God wants to drill a man,
And thrill a man,
And skill a man;
When God wants to mold a man
To play the noblest part,
Then he yearns with all his heart
To create so great and bold a man
That all the world shall be amazed,
Watch his methods, watch his ways—
How he ruthlessly perfects
Whom he royally elects.
How he hammers him and hurts him,
And with mighty blows, converts him
Into trial shapes of clay
Which only God understands.
While his tortured heart is crying,
And he lifts beseeching hands.
How he bends but never breaks
When his good he undertakes.
How he uses Whom he chooses,

And with every purpose, fuses him,
By every act, induces him
To try his splendor out.
God knows what he's about.

(We need to fully grasp what this poet did, God is at work, He has a
purpose, and *He knows what He's doing.*)

One of God's primary purposes for our storms
that we *can* understand is: He wants to conform us
into the likeness of Christ.

For those God foreknew he also predestined to be con-
formed to the likeness of his Son, that he might be the
firstborn among many brothers. (Romans 8:29 NIV)

He is molding us, so that our character mirrors that
of Jesus: the way He thinks, loves, and forgives.
Through the process, He is teaching us to depend
on His presence, instead of relying on our own
strength. We are to draw *all* of our strength from
Him.

I am the vine; you are the branches.
If a man remains in me and I in him,
he will bear much fruit;
apart from me you can do nothing.
(John 15:5 NIV)

As God works on our character, He uses our suffering to teach us to keep focused upon Him. God's incredible love for us does not eliminate the pain, suffering, and heartache that we might go through; but, His Promises assure us that He is with us, and He is using it all for good (Romans 8:28).

Through it all, we learn to trust that no matter how devastating the storm might be…God is with us. And if we trust and obey Him, He will strengthen us and fill us with hope in the *midst* of the storm.

We do not know what to do, but our eyes are upon you.
(2 Chronicles 20:12 NIV)

You see, His presence is made perfect in your weakness; it is in your weakest moments where He will comfort you, strengthen you, and reassure you of His faithfulness. He wants you to know that He is not in your life to stop the storms from coming, but to take you through them. *He wants your faith.*

And it is impossible to please God without faith.
Anyone who wants to come to him must believe
that God exists and that he rewards
those who sincerely seek him.
(Hebrews 11:6 NLT)

God's Presence in the Storm

We can be certain that God would never test our faith and then push us out to sea without His presence. The question is, "Do *you* acknowledge His presence during these storms of life?" The even greater question is, *"At what point* do you acknowledge His presence?" We storm the gates of heaven, wondering, *"Where is God?"* Yet, we fail to see that He is there with us...*and He's been there all along.* In fact, He's in the clouds—He's hovering over us each day, going before us, preparing a way through the storm.

The cloud of the Lord was over them
by day when they set out from the camp.
(Numbers 10:34 NIV)

They have heard that You, O Lord, are in the midst of
this people, for You, O Lord, are seen eye to eye, while
Your cloud stands over them; and You go before them in
a pillar of cloud by day and in a pillar of fire by night.
(Numbers 14:14 NASB)

Just think about the fact that the Disciples were in a boat, with who they supposedly believed was the Son of God; yet, even *they* failed to acknowledge Him, until it was almost too late. They were about to die! Why didn't it occur to them to ask for Jesus' help sooner? From the outside looking in, the answer seemed so obvious. In our own storms of life, it's often difficult to see the "obvious." Our vision becomes clouded with debilitating doubt and paralyzing fear.

The Disciples had seen Jesus perform many miracles — we have seen God work miracles in our own lives, yet we so easily forget them. Jesus says, *"Don't you remember?"* (Matthew 16:9) If they had faith in Him, the answer would be obvious — ask the Son of God to calm the storm! But they didn't. God knew that the Disciples' faith would grow through this experience. Their greater faith would enable them to be better witnesses. The miracles He performed were to teach us to have faith in Him, regardless of our circumstances — no matter how impossible things might seem. God reminds us through His Word:

Everything is possible for him who believes.
(Mark 9:23 NIV)

Have faith in God.
(Mark 11:22 NIV)

The message God has for *you* is no different than it was for the Disciples. He wants you to know that faith in Him can bring about miracles in your life.

Many of us believe that miracles won't happen to us. Or maybe we're like the Disciples and we think that we have the ability to make it through this storm on our own. But, when we can't seem to rescue ourselves, we finally, as a last ditch effort, ask for God's help. Hear this truth: *"You don't have to save yourself."* (Besides, you can't!) Jesus came so that you don't have to...*He's the one who saves you through every storm of life.* He is all you need.

We tend to wait until the last moment because we seem to think that God can't possibly intervene in our situation. How much peace do we forfeit by struggling for the answers on our own? How much pain do we needlessly bear because we agonize over possibilities that never happen? We tend to believe that there are some things that God can handle, but we're convinced that on many things...*He needs our help.* At other times, we're certain that it's necessary for us to take control...God just seems to be taking too long. Even the Disciples, at some point, subconsciously believed that there was nothing that Jesus could do to help them calm the wind and waves of the storm. It was the perfect set up for the perfect miracle. ***God knows what He's doing.***

In the storm, He's bringing us to a place of embracing the truth that our life is better managed by His hands, not our own. Trust Him—He does a much better job than we could ever do.

When miracles happen,
hope destroys hopelessness,
joy overcomes pain, love conquers hate,
and faith finds God in the midst of it all.

In the face of impossible circumstances, God says, "Lift up your eyes. Look beyond the visible realities." God doesn't work in the "natural." He works in the "*super*natural." His only requirement is that we no longer be "unbelieving," but "believing." He says, "*Believe and have faith that I am at work,* and I will enrich your life beyond your imagination." Do you dare believe God? When miracles happen, hope destroys hopelessness, joy overcomes pain, love conquers hate, and *faith finds God in the midst of it all*...ever present...worthy of praise.

Who doesn't want a miracle? Who doesn't want to be saved from the paralyzing grip of fear? We beg God for a miracle, but when He shows up, we're often found with very little faith—we're like the Disciples, standing in awe and amazement. Our faith should never be surprised to see God's hand, when we've come to a place of surrender.

In our world, becoming mature means becoming "independent." In our spiritual journey, maturity means becoming *helplessly dependent upon God*. Our peace in the storm can only come from our resignation into God's hands. Regardless of how hopeless a situation might seem, we must surrender all of our hopes and expectations into His hands; when we do, we find that He will empower us to endure any hardship. His desire is that we would continue the journey without fear or anxiety, while trusting in His care. The more resigned we are to God's care, the less power our circumstances have over us. When we're resigned to God's care, we won't be frightened by undesirable news, and we won't be trying to constantly figure out the next step. If we have faith in God, we will simply trust, wait, and *expect* God.

Such people will not be overcome by evil.
Those who are righteous will be long remembered.
THEY DO NOT FEAR BAD NEWS;
 they confidently trust the LORD to care for them.
THEY ARE CONFIDENT AND FEARLESS AND
CAN FACE THEIR FOES TRIUMPHANTLY.
(Psalm 112:6-8 NLT)

Quite possibly, you're not sure that you want to take that step. You might feel that "trusting God" comes with too much obligation. You might decide that you don't want to feel a burden of having to "repay" God for His miracle in your life. You may desire His hand, but you're not sure about coming face to face with Him (Job 23:15). You may be overwhelmed in feeling that you would be in debt to Him and you don't want to carry that weight. The truth is that you're already in deeper debt to Him than you'll ever imagine; that's why He sent Jesus. *Jesus can save you.* It's the storms of your life that bring you to a place of surrender. God wants you to stop all of your "trying" and simply start "trusting." He wants to eliminate the fleshly part of you that wants to control your life. He wants you to encounter something much more wonderful than anything you could devise. When you truly understand your storms of life, you will find that your storms will allow God to lift you up and give you true life to the full...*until it overflows.*

It's possible that if we never had to face our storms of life, we wouldn't seek the Lord. The purpose of your storm, simply put, is all about your relationship with Jesus. It's all out your faith in Him.

In John Ortberg's book, *"Faith and Doubt,"* he defines our faith and hope by saying that, *"Hope points to one Man, one hope, one God who is worth trusting, not because of who He is. He is the one in whom and by whom we can hope."* Faith looks Jesus in the eyes and says, *"Yes Lord, wherever You lead...I will follow."* We can trust that if He leads us into a raging storm, or allows a storm to come into our lives, He's got something amazing in mind. He wants to show you His sufficiency, His comforting presence, and His strength that will help you endure. Your *trials* become *tools* in the hand of God. Tell Him you'll follow Him — *then watch Him go to work.*

Then Jesus said to the Disciples, "If any of you wants to be my follower, you must put aside your selfish ambition, shoulder your cross and follow me. If you try to keep your life for yourself, you will lose it. But if you give up your life for me, you will find true life." (Mark 8:34-35 NLT)

When you bow down before the Lord and admit your dependence on him, he will lift you up and give you honor. (James 4:10 NLT)

The Call of the Storm

Storms of life are used by God to strengthen your faith in Him. He's asking you to step out in faith and show Him that you are ready to live with Him forever. The storms call us to a higher place — they prove our faith and mature us spiritually. God may or may not have sent the storm into our life, but we can rest assured that He is with us through it all. The more we trust Him, the more our faith will grow. Placing our trust in Him will make all the difference for the journey.

Don't make the mistake of basing your faith on a particular outcome. We've all done it. We've prayed for God to answer our prayers with very detailed expectations, and we've seen our faith crumble to pieces when things didn't happen the way we thought they should. We find ourselves embracing "positive thinking," instead of real faith. Faith that grows us trusts in "Someone" rather than "something." Faith trusts in the character of God who is merciful, loving, and just. God doesn't ask us to "blindly" trust Him. He reveals Himself through Scripture and through our experiences to convince us that He *is* trustworthy.

The call of the storms in your life is to have greater faith in God. Your circumstances might look hopeless, you may have cried out to God for help, and you may have only heard a deafening silence; but, in your moments of abandoning all hope, you will find yourself in awe and amazement when you witness the power of God in your life. Your momentary pain and suffering will vanish, in an instant, when you open your soul to the risks of faith. Faith in God will bring you to the edge...*every time*. Each step of faith will demand that you reach out for the hand of God. He wants you to be a witness to His awesome presence and power.

The call of the storm in the Disciples' lives

caused them to be devoted witnesses to Christ because they experienced a "personal" miracle through the magnificent power of God—Jesus calmed their storm...He saved their lives.

Then Jesus told him, "You believe because you have seen
me. Blessed are those who haven't seen me
and believe anyway."
(John 20:29 NLT)

When trying to understand how this miracle relates to your life and the storms you face, it is important to realize that the storm did not slowly subside or die down—when the Disciples cried out to Jesus for help...it stopped immediately! It appears that from that moment on, the Disciples were overwhelmed, not only with the power that Jesus possessed, but that He truly must be the Son of God. When the Disciples witnessed this great miracle, they were suddenly overcome by its "stillness." Imagine being more frightened of how your storm of life is "stilled," rather than of the fear of the raging storm itself!

Behind every storm there is a blessing.
View your storm as a revelation from God,
an opportunity to learn to trust Him,
and a stepping stone for better things in the future.

Can you imagine? Whatever storm you're currently in, God can stop it *immediately*.

When we call upon the name of Jesus, He does hear us; He will answer us through the storm. Will you call upon Him now? Will you show Him your faith in Him and cry out to Him even when you cannot see Him? *Or will you keep trying to bail water out of a boat that is already capsizing?*

The Disciples were truly the closest men to the Son of God; yet, at the end of this miracle we see that *even they* had doubts in their heart about who Jesus really was. They saw with their own eyes all of the miracles He performed, but they still asked, *"Who is this man?"* A little surprising...don't you think? Onlookers may have believed that the Disciples must have had the highest level of faith—they left their lives and followed Jesus. But, Jesus knew where their faith was lacking. Jesus saw their hearts...just like He sees yours. You cannot hide your heart from God.

It is in our storms where the areas of our lives that are hindering our spiritual growth are revealed. It is in the storms that God will reveal, refine, strengthen, and perfect those areas...if you allow Him to take you through the storm.

You can trust God. He already knows exactly what He's going to do in your situation. He has a plan. He wants you to place your trust in Him by saying, "You are God, and nothing is impossible with You. I am giving this situation to You and it is no longer mine but yours to deal with as You will. "He's taking your faith to a place of understanding His desire and ability to work a miracle for you—not only in your current storm, but in every storm you will ever face. His desire is that you would develop an un-wavering faith that is *anchored* in Him.

Trust in, lean on, rely on, and have confidence in Him at all times, you people; pour out your hearts before Him.
God is a refuge for us (a fortress and a high tower).
Selah [pause, and calmly think of that]!
(Psalm 62:8 AMP)

The Blessing Behind the Storm

It should be comforting to know that although God allows the storm, Jesus is in the boat with you. Yes, He is with you, right now, in the boat where you sit in the midst of your storm. The difference is: He is in the stern resting because He knows the blessing behind all of the wind and rain. He knows that the destruction in your life can be used to rebuild your life and make it better than it was before. He knows that God has the power to turn your ashes to beauty.

To all who mourn in Israel, he will give beauty for ashes, joy instead of mourning, praise instead of despair. For the Lord has planted them strong and graceful oaks for his own glory. (Isaiah 61:3 NLT)

There is no storm that is not permitted and controlled by God. When Jesus rose from the dead, He overcame every spirit in opposition to Him. By His resurrection, Jesus proclaimed power over all demonic forces in your life. This means that whatever your storm is, God has allowed it, and it has been overcome through Christ — just knowing this should bring about a great blessing in your spirit. Behind every storm there is a blessing — God has assured us there is one. Why not view this time as a revelation from God, an opportunity to learn to trust Him, and a stepping stone to better things in the future. He's assured us:

God blesses the people who patiently endure testing.
(James 1:12 NLT)

For the Disciples, their blessing was acquiring greater faith in God which made them the greatest witnesses for Christ — what a blessing for you and I! When God allows a storm in your life…it has great purpose; if you miss the purpose, you may miss God's will for your life.

Every intimate part of our lives is no surprise to God. Many times, when He leads us into the storms, He's leading us to a place of surrender and complete dependence upon Him. The storms aren't necessarily to show us His incredible powers; although His love, mercy, and grace continually amaze even those with incredible faith. God doesn't have to prove His power, just as He doesn't have to prove His existence—it's the obvious. We just have to open our eyes and look around us. We don't have to go very far to realize there is an amazing God who keeps the world in motion, and He has addressed every intricate detail which sustains life here on earth.

God is more interested in showing us the heart of who He is. God wants us to understand that our storms are more than just storms. They are more than just the pain and suffering on the surface. Our storms build a bridge to an intimate relationship with Him. The storms just give God another opportunity to demonstrate His unconditional love for us.

He wants you to understand, firsthand, what it feels like to reach out and have His hand grasp yours. He wants you to understand what it's like to see His face and hear His voice. No one and nothing can simply give you this intimate understanding through witnessing. Others' relationship with God can you *lead* you to Him, but He does the rest. God wants a very personal relationship with you…He wants you to experience a miracle *in your own life.* The Disciples had witnessed many miracles that Jesus had performed, yet they had not experienced a miracle for themselves; when Jesus calmed the storm, they were given a "personal" miracle.

God wants to give you greater knowledge of Himself, so that when the storms rage around you, you can have peace because you have learned that He is in control and there is nothing to fear. He wants you to be assured that He is with you, He will carry you, and He is your refuge and source of strength.

You can rest assured through God's Promises that He will use every storm for your good and His greater purposes. God always has a plan. Trust Him— get to the back of the boat with Jesus.

God is our refuge and strength, always ready to help in times of trouble. (Psalm 46:1 NLT)

When you understand your storms and grasp the fact that Jesus is in your boat, you, too, can experience a miracle in your storm. When you seek out God's call to you through the storm, allowing Him to use it all for His purposes, your storms will bring about great blessings in your life. You'll even find that your storms of life will be used by God to bless the lives of others! You can rest assured through God's Promises...He will use *every* storm for your good and His greater purposes. God always has a plan. Trust Him. It's your life He wants to use, but He can't use you unless you're in the *back* of the boat with Jesus—at rest, trusting Him. So, the begging question is:

"Where are you in the boat right now?"

Scriptures to Encourage You in the Storm

These trials are only to test your faith, to show that it is strong and pure. It is being tested as fire tests and purifies gold — and your faith is far more precious to God than mere gold. So if your faith remains strong after being tried by fiery trials, it will bring you much praise and glory and honor on the day when Jesus Christ is revealed to the whole world. (1 Peter 1:7 NLT)

So, be truly glad! There is wonderful joy ahead, even though it is necessary for you to endure many trials for a while.(1 Peter 1:6 NLT)

I know the Lord is always with me. I will not be shaken, for he is right beside me. (Psalm 16:8 NLT)

So be strong and take courage, all you who put your hope in the Lord! (Psalm 31:24 NLT)

"For I know the plans I have for you," says the Lord. "They are plans for good and not for disaster, to give you a future and a hope. In those days when you pray, I will listen. If you look for me in earnest, you will find me when you seek me." (Jeremiah 29:11 NLT)

Draw close to God, and God will draw close to you.
(James 4:8 NLT)

We can rejoice, too, when we run into problems and trials, for we know that they are good for us – they help us learn strength of character in us, and character strengthens our confident expectations of salvation. And this expectation will not disappoint us for we know how dearly God loves us, because he has given us the Holy Spirit to fill our hearts with his love. (Romans 5:3 NLT)

So let us come boldly to the throne of our gracious God. There we will receive his mercy, and we will find grace to help us when we need it. (Hebrews 4:16 NLT)

God is our refuge and strength, always ready to help in times of trouble. (Psalm 46:1 NLT)

I have refined you but not in the way silver is refined. Rather, I have refined you in the furnace of suffering. I will rescue you for my sake, – yes, for my own sake! (Isaiah 48:10 NLT)

We are pressed on every side by troubles, but we are not crushed and broken. We are perplexed, but we don't give up and quit. We are hunted down, but God never abandons us. We get knocked down, but we get up again and keep going… (2 Corinthians 4: 8-10 NLT)

For you will rescue me from my troubles and help me to triumph … (Psalm 54:7 NLT)

So humble yourselves under the mighty power of God, and in his good time he will honor you. Give all your worries and cares to God, for he cares about what happens to you. (1 Peter 5:6-7 NLT)

Do not fear anything except the Lord Almighty. He alone is the Holy one. If you fear him, you need fear nothing else. He will keep you safe.
(Isaiah 8: 12-14 NLT)

In quietness and in trusting confidence I find strength.
(Isaiah 30:15 NLT)

It was by faith that Moses left the land of Egypt, not fearing the king's anger. He kept right on going because he kept his eyes on the one who is invisible.
(Hebrews 11:27-28 NLT)

We do not know what to do, but our eyes are upon you.
(2 Chronicles 20:12 NLT)

In quietness and confidence is your strength.
(Isaiah 30:15 NLT)

About the Author

*Cherie Hill is the founder of ScriptureNow.com Ministry
which brings the Word of God into over
30 countries around the world.*

*She has a BA in Psychology and is trained in
Biblical Counseling through the AACC.
She is an Amazon.com Bestselling Christian Living author,
ranked in the top 10 authors for Religion and Spirituality,
who spends her time at the feet of Jesus.*

Bestselling Author of:

WAITING on GOD

Hope Being Gone

BE STILL
(Let Jesus Calm Your Storms)

Beginning at The End
(Finding God When Your World Falls Apart)

THE WAYS of GOD
(Finding Purpose Through Your Pain)

empty.
(Living Full of Faith When Life Drains You Dry)

FAITH Under Construction

Made in the USA
Coppell, TX
07 November 2021

65327088R00068